Praise for The Write H

"I used to think that writing must be hard... A 'true writer' sacrifices family time, sleep, and sometimes sanity, right? Dr Nicole Janz turns that myth upside down and asks: What if writing could be easy? I couldn't agree more, and I'm excited to see this idea executed in *The Write Habit* planner.
With clear and simple planning sheets, the workbook helps you prioritise your writing and rally support around yourself - to make writing flow effortless. Stop trying so hard. Start using the planner and find easier ways to write every single week."

— **Greg McKeown**, author of the NYT bestsellers *Essentialism* and *Effortless*, and host of *The Greg McKeown Podcast.*

"Wanting to write is the easy part; committing to write is the real challenge. *The Write Habit* equips you with the structure, tools, and prompts to make committing to your writing feel fun and a lot more doable. Pick it up, keep it on your desk, and be amazed at your progress."

— **Matt Trinetti & Parul Bavishi,** Co-Founders of *London Writers' Salon*

"A perfect writerly companion - especially for those who suffer from perfectionism and procrastination - I wish I'd had this book before getting published!"

— **Menna Van Praag**, author of the fantasy trilogy *The Sisters Grimm, Night of Demons and Saints, & Child of Earth and Sky*

"The Write Habit planner is the best tool I've seen to get into writing flow fast. Dr Janz masterfully weaves the latest research on the Future Self into a simple, actionable tool that reshapes how writers prioritise their goals and make space for creativity. Grab this planner now and watch your confidence grow, propelling you towards your envisioned Future Self—a thriving, prolific writer."

— **Dr Benjamin Hardy**, organizational psychologist and best-selling author of *Be Your Future Self Now, 10X Is Easier Than 2X,* and *Willpower Doesn't Work.*

"Simple and to the point - the planner keeps me focused!"

— **Scott Proposki,** former White House photographer, business coach; author of *Bee Focused* and Amazon bestseller *Camera Focus*

"Dr Nicole Janz balances accountability and grace in a way that few writing coaches can. Her expertise in keeping writers writing—and writing well—is embedded throughout *The Write Habit* planner, which should be the first resource in any writer's toolkit!"

— **Brannan Sirratt,** Developmental Editor, Ghostwriter, and Author of *You Don't Get to the Ocean By Accident*

"I just wanted to say how freaking AWESOME this planner is! I'm going to share it with my postgrad students, too!"

— **Dr Katrina McChesney**, Senior Lecturer, University of Waikato

"**This is an excellent tool for making small changes with big results, designed specifically for writers.** *The Write Habit* planner doesn't tell you what to do—it asks you what you want to do, and then helps you do it. Dr Nicole Janz's insightful questions invite you to figure out what matters most to you, what's in the way, and how you're going to make room for small steps that will eventually add up to a journey you're proud of."

— **Emily Winslow,** author of a series of Cambridge-set crime novels, the memoir *Jane Doe January*, & the writing guide *Time to Write*

"**As writers, we rely on two motivational drivers:** the pull to create and the push that comes from within to get the job done. This planner is our friend and guide. It offers focus, direction, structure and self-discipline, all couched in a practical, reassuring, encouraging tone designed to boost our self-belief and give us the push we need."

— **Derek Niemann**, author of *A Nazi in the Family* and *Birds in a Cage*, *Guardian* country diary columnist and creative writing tutor at the University of Cambridge

"**Dr Nicole Janz has brought together the most powerful elements in creating and sustaining a writing habit in one elegant, practical planner.** From the 'Future Self' perspective to the 10-minute rule, it's everything you need to stop procrastinating and start writing consistently. Genius!"

— **Alison Jones**, founder and director of *Practical Inspiration Publishing*, host of the *Extraordinary Business Book Club* podcast and author of *Exploratory Writing*

"**Dr Nicole Janz's process has been a game changer for me**. I use her steps weekly to create my newsletter; from this newsletter, I pull a lot more content for other social media platforms and my podcast. The tools are the foundation of my weekly process. If you are feeling stuck, you need *The Write Habit* planner in your life."

— **Stephen Timoney**, High-Performance coach & host of the Self-Performance Strategies Podcast, www.stephentimoney.com

"**My relationship with writing has changed completely!** In my experience, Dr Nicole Janz is the best writing coach out there. "

— **Dr Jutta Tobias Mortlock**, Senior Lecturer in Organisational Psychology, City University of London

"**The Write Habit Planner is the gift that keeps on giving.** It's the most useful planner! It's clear and comprehensive - no stone is left unturned. It's is a godsend to writers of all genres. As a freelance copywriter I found I was focussing all my efforts on writing for my clients and not spending enough time on content writing to market my own business.
Working through the planner has given me valuable headspace to prioritise and plan my writing projects in a way that is manageable and sustainable. I've referred to it over and over again - It keeps me on track and helps me stay focused on my goals."

— **Ella Hoyos,** Conversion Copywriter, www.flurrymarketing.com

The Write Habit

Set better goals

Optimise your flow

Write daily with ease

Name ______________________________

Email ______________________________

Mobile ______________________________

Before you start using *The Write Habit*, close your eyes and picture yourself a year from today.

You wake up in the morning, and your writing is published.

Your story, research and expertise have reached their audience, and the feedback has been amazing.

All of your procrastination and worry is gone.

You have become a successful writer.

And best of all, you found writing one of the easiest processes you've ever had.

Let's get started and turn YOUR VISION into reality!

Your coach,

Dr Nicole Janz

Find tips, training & planning tools at

THEWRITEHABITPLANNER.COM/GETSTARTED

Creativity Contract

I, ______________________

am fully committed to my writing goals.

I prioritise my projects. I avoid distractions. I set clear goals and stay on track.

In a year from now, my Future Self will be proud of me.

I'm ready for writing flow!

Sign ______________________

Date ______________________

How it Works

How do I go from stuck and overwhelmed to writing daily with ease? *The Write Habit* has been designed to help you do just that! You will learn to set better writing goals, get into flow state, and create a daily writing habit.

1 PLAN WITH YOUR FUTURE SELF

Set more meaningful writing goals *from* your Future Self.

- Who do you want to be?
- What publications are key?
- What habits will get you there?

This helps you clarify your vision, get motivated, and connect deeply with your writing.

2 BREAK DOWN THE MOUNTAIN

Write down your goals for the year and break them down to:

- Create small action steps
- Always know where to start
- Foresee obstacles and solutions

In the coming months and weeks you'll reflect and re-set this roadmap to stay on track when life gets busy.

3 SET 3 PRIORITIES

Each quarter, each month, and each week, you will identify your 'big 3' goals that matter the most so you:

- Use your time more intentionally
- Drop endless to-do lists
- Enjoy a more spacious schedule

Every week, you will allocate specific time slots in your schedule for your 'big 3' so they get done!

4 USE WRITING SLOTS EFFECTIVELY

You will plan which writing-related activities you will focus on each month, week and day, e.g.

- Prepare, read, plan
- Draft new content without editing
- Edit, revise, or proofread

You'll get into the habit of being intentional about your tasks and 'wear only one hat at a time'.

What would you create if writing was easy?

5 ACCOUNTABILITY

Consistently monitor your daily achievements and note significant insights about your writing routine:

- Track your daily targets & wins
- Assess your weekly productivity
- Reflect each month and re-commit

By measuring successes and lessons, failures turn into growth and you stay motivated to keep writing!

6 WRITER'S TOOLBOX

Use the 5 tools at the back of the planner when you get stuck or want to deepen your habits, e.g.

- Create your own Flow Ritual
- Master the art of saying 'no'
- Try our 12 ways out of block

Consider this toolbox your self-coaching and support system for whenever you need it.

Find tips, training & planning tools at

THEWRITEHABITPLANNER.COM/GETSTARTED

HOW TO USE YOUR GOAL PAGES

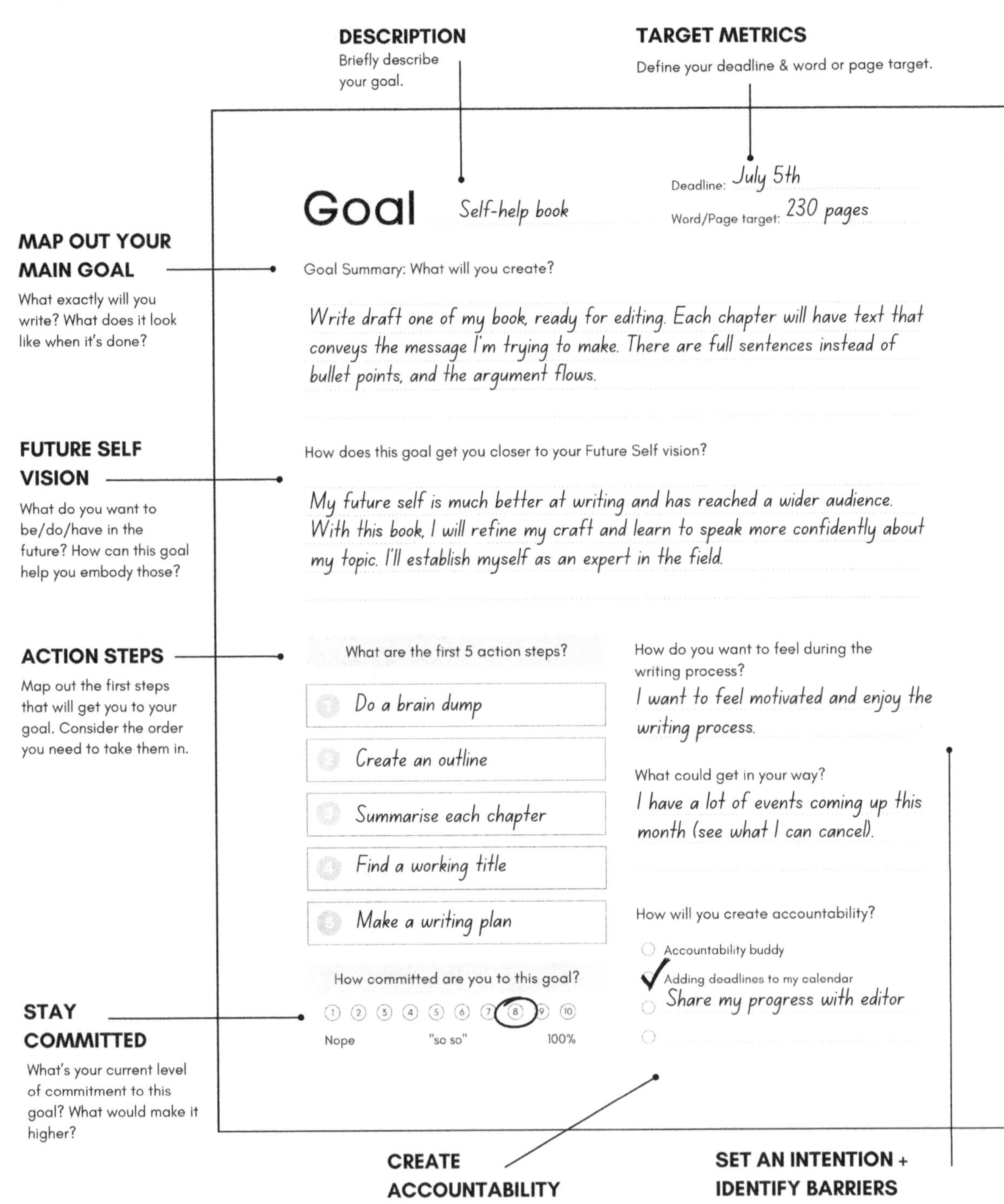

DESCRIPTION
Briefly describe your goal.

TARGET METRICS
Define your deadline & word or page target.

MAP OUT YOUR MAIN GOAL
What exactly will you write? What does it look like when it's done?

FUTURE SELF VISION
What do you want to be/do/have in the future? How can this goal help you embody those?

ACTION STEPS
Map out the first steps that will get you to your goal. Consider the order you need to take them in.

STAY COMMITTED
What's your current level of commitment to this goal? What would make it higher?

CREATE ACCOUNTABILITY
Who or what will help you write consistently?

SET AN INTENTION + IDENTIFY BARRIERS
Set an intention for how you want to feel and identify possible roadblocks.

GOAL DATES
Mark down when you will start and complete your goal.

Goal Roadmap

Jan 3rd — Start

July 5th — End

Use this page to create a realistic timeline, milestones & reflection points.

Visual timeline

Note your start & end date for the project. Then, add 2-5 big milestones & dates along the way.

Jan	Feb	March	April	May	June	July
Plan + Ch 1	Ch 2	Ch 3	Ch 4	Ch 5	Read + revise	Send to editor

VISUAL MILESTONES
Map out the milestones you will work towards.

Realistic timeframe

Step 1: Use your calendar to count how many days/weeks you have from start to finish.
Tip: If you count days, work with half days (2-3h block) vs. full days (4-6h block).

ca. 180 — Available days

Step 2: Deduct holidays, travel, recovery time, or busy weeks from the above number.

ca. 165 — Realistic days

SET REALISTIC EXPECTATIONS
How many days will you actually be able to work on your goal?

Bullet-proof the roadmap

Are you confident you can finish this goal on time? If not, which of the following options might help?

- ○ Move the deadline
- ○ Start earlier
- ○ Hire help
- ○ Reduce the scope
- ✓ Remove competing tasks
- ○ Delegate parts of this goal
- ✓ writing retreats
- ○
- ○

CREATE A SUCCESS PATH
Take these steps to ensure you reach your goal on time.

Plan your reflection

I will reflect on my progress and adjust my roadmap on: 15 Feb — Date

PLAN TO REVIEW
Set a time to reflect on your progress.

HOW TO USE YOUR WEEKLY SPREADS

TIMEFRAME

Write down this week's date.

MAP OUT YOUR MAIN GOALS

What are your 'big 3' goals for the week ahead? These can be different projects, or your main task broken down into 3 parts.

TASKS, EVENTS, DEADLINES

Write down important details you mustn't forget this week.

HABIT FOCUS & RELEASE

Identify your main habit focus for the week & what you want to release, let go of, or say no to.

QUICK REFLECT

Jot down 3 highlights or learning moments from the week.

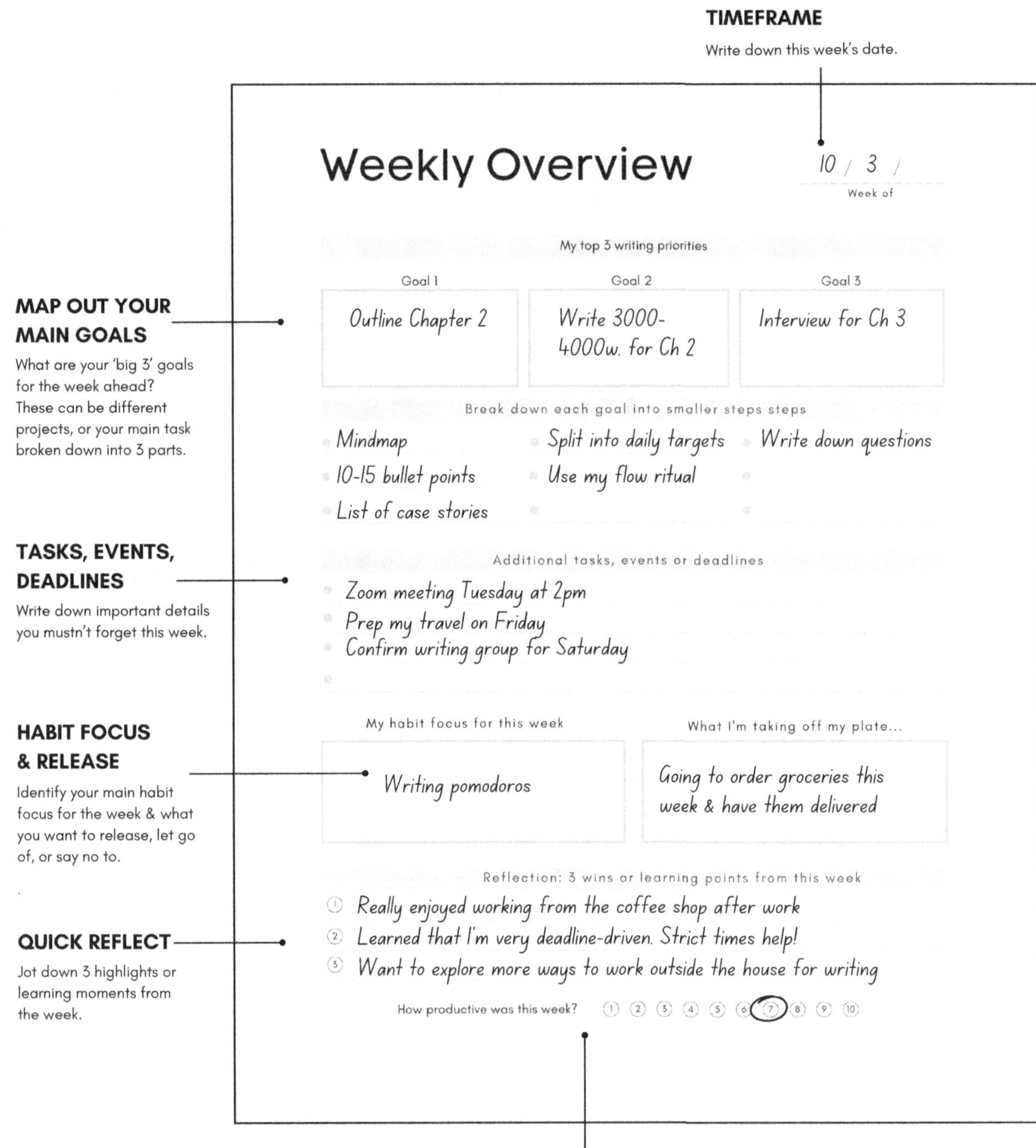

RATE YOUR PRODUCTIVITY

How do you feel about what you were able to get done?

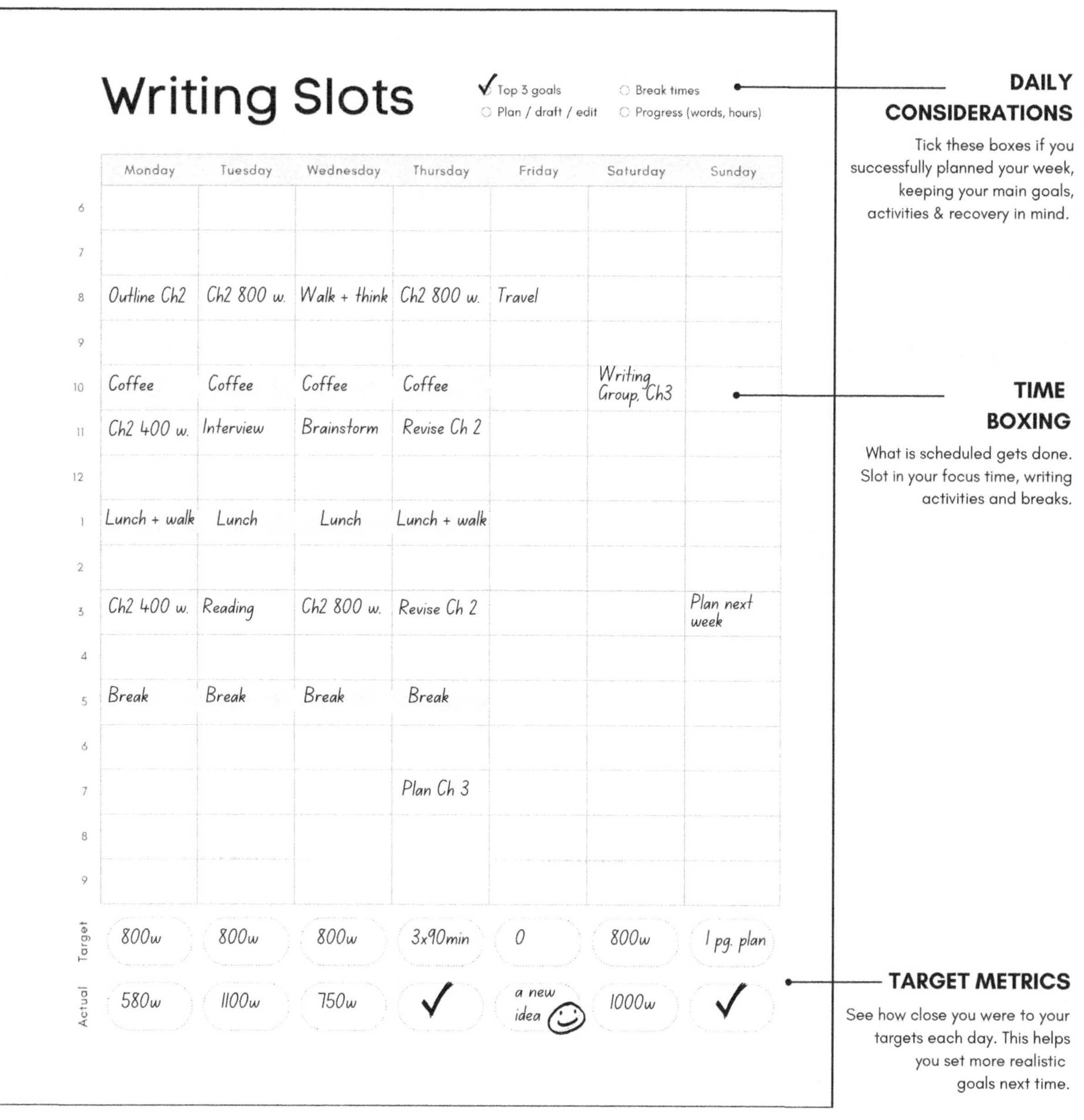

DAILY CONSIDERATIONS

Tick these boxes if you successfully planned your week, keeping your main goals, activities & recovery in mind.

TIME BOXING

What is scheduled gets done. Slot in your focus time, writing activities and breaks.

TARGET METRICS

See how close you were to your targets each day. This helps you set more realistic goals next time.

"Keep some blank spots on your calendar. Room for stillness. Ideas love to visit when you're at ease."

— Dr Nicole Janz

Review Your Past

What are your creative wins of the last 12 months? Think of all your outputs, but also moments you wrote in flow or found great collaborators. List small and big wins.

What didn't work for you in the past? Where did you get stuck or frustrated?

If you could thank yourself for all the efforts and learnings, what would you say?

Dear Past Me, thank you for...

Your Future Self Vision

What are your creative dreams for the next 12 months? What will you publish?

How would your life be different if you achieved these goals?

What key skills, people or habits will help you get there?

To turn my Future Self vision into reality ...

I'll stop...

I'll start ...

Annual Goals

Step 1: Top 3-5 writing priorities for the next 12 months

-
-
-
-
-

Step 2: Other goals, events & deadlines

Rank importance

Step 3: Break down your top goals

For your top goals, spend time on planning out the action steps & your timeline using the tools in this planner:

→ "Goal"
→ "Goal Roadmap"

Quarterly Focus

Break down your top goals and deadlines and plan them across the upcoming quarters.

Quarter 1	Month
	J F M
	J F M
	J F M

Quarter 2	
	A M J
	A M J
	A M J

Quarter 3	
	J A S
	J A S
	J A S

Quarter 4	
	O N D
	O N D
	O N D

Goal

Deadline:

Word/Page target:

Goal Summary: What will you create?

How does this goal get you closer to your Future Self vision?

What are the first 5 action steps?

1

2

3

4

5

How committed are you to this goal?

① ② ③ ④ ⑤ ⑥ ⑦ ⑧ ⑨ ⑩

Nope "So so" 100%

How do you want to feel during the writing process?

What could get in your way?

How will you create accountability?

- ○ Accountability buddy
- ○ Adding deadlines to my calendar
- ○
- ○

Goal Roadmap

_/_/_ Start _/_/_ End

Use this page to create a realistic timeline, milestones & reflection points.

Visual timeline

Note your start & end date for the project. Then, add 2-5 big milestones & dates along the way.

Realistic timeframe

Step 1: Use your calendar to count how many days/weeks you have from start to finish.
Tip: If you count days, work with half days (2-3h block) vs. full days (4-6h block).

Available days

Step 2: Deduct holidays, travel, recovery time, or busy weeks from the above number.

Realistic days

Bullet-proof the roadmap

Are you confident you can finish this goal on time? If not, which of the following options might help?

- ○ Move the deadline
- ○ Start earlier
- ○ Hire help
- ○ Reduce the scope
- ○ Remove competing tasks
- ○ Delegate parts of this goal
- ○
- ○
- ○

Plan your reflection

I will reflect on my progress and adjust my roadmap on:

_/_/_ Date

Goal

Deadline:

Word/Page target:

Goal Summary: What will you create?

How does this goal get you closer to your Future Self vision?

What are the first 5 action steps?

1.
2.
3.
4.
5.

How committed are you to this goal?

① ② ③ ④ ⑤ ⑥ ⑦ ⑧ ⑨ ⑩

Nope "So so" 100%

How do you want to feel during the writing process?

What could get in your way?

How will you create accountability?

- ○ Accountability buddy
- ○ Adding deadlines to my calendar
- ○
- ○

Goal Roadmap

/ /
Start

/ /
End

Use this page to create a realistic timeline, milestones & reflection points.

Visual timeline

Note your start & end date for the project. Then, add 2-5 big milestones & dates along the way.

Realistic timeframe

Step 1: Use your calendar to count how many days/weeks you have from start to finish.
Tip: If you count days, work with half days (2-3h block) vs. full days (4-6h block).

Available days

Step 2: Deduct holidays, travel, recovery time, or busy weeks from the above number.

Realistic days

Bullet-proof the roadmap

Are you confident you can finish this goal on time? If not, which of the following options might help?

- ○ Move the deadline
- ○ Reduce the scope
- ○
- ○ Start earlier
- ○ Remove competing tasks
- ○
- ○ Hire help
- ○ Delegate parts of this goal
- ○

Plan your reflection

I will reflect on my progress and adjust my roadmap on:

/ /
Date

Goal

Deadline:

Word/Page target:

Goal Summary: What will you create?

How does this goal get you closer to your Future Self vision?

What are the first 5 action steps?

1
2
3
4
5

How committed are you to this goal?

① ② ③ ④ ⑤ ⑥ ⑦ ⑧ ⑨ ⑩

Nope "So so" 100%

How do you want to feel during the writing process?

What could get in your way?

How will you create accountability?

- ○ Accountability buddy
- ○ Adding deadlines to my calendar
- ○
- ○

Goal Roadmap

/ / Start

/ / End

Use this page to create a realistic timeline, milestones & reflection points.

Visual timeline

Note your start & end date for the project. Then, add 2-5 big milestones & dates along the way.

Realistic timeframe

Step 1: Use your calendar to count how many days/weeks you have from start to finish.
Tip: If you count days, work with half days (2-3h block) vs. full days (4-6h block).

Available days

Step 2: Deduct holidays, travel, recovery time, or busy weeks from the above number.

Realistic days

Bullet-proof the roadmap

Are you confident you can finish this goal on time? If not, which of the following options might help?

- ○ Move the deadline
- ○ Start earlier
- ○ Hire help
- ○ Reduce the scope
- ○ Remove competing tasks
- ○ Delegate parts of this goal
- ○
- ○
- ○

Plan your reflection

I will reflect on my progress and adjust my roadmap on:

/ / Date

Goal

Deadline:

Word/Page target:

Goal Summary: What will you create?

How does this goal get you closer to your Future Self vision?

What are the first 5 action steps?

1.
2.
3.
4.
5.

How committed are you to this goal?

① ② ③ ④ ⑤ ⑥ ⑦ ⑧ ⑨ ⑩

Nope "So so" 100%

How do you want to feel during the writing process?

What could get in your way?

How will you create accountability?

- ○ Accountability buddy
- ○ Adding deadlines to my calendar
- ○
- ○

Goal Roadmap

/ / Start

/ / End

Use this page to create a realistic timeline, milestones & reflection points.

Visual timeline

Note your start & end date for the project. Then, add 2-5 big milestones & dates along the way.

Realistic timeframe

Step 1: Use your calendar to count how many days/weeks you have from start to finish.
Tip: If you count days, work with half days (2-3h block) vs. full days (4-6h block).

Available days

Step 2: Deduct holidays, travel, recovery time, or busy weeks from the above number.

Realistic days

Bullet-proof the roadmap

Are you confident you can finish this goal on time? If not, which of the following options might help?

- ○ Move the deadline
- ○ Start earlier
- ○ Hire help
- ○ Reduce the scope
- ○ Remove competing tasks
- ○ Delegate parts of this goal
- ○
- ○
- ○

Plan your reflection

I will reflect on my progress and adjust my roadmap on:

/ / Date

Goal

Deadline:

Word/Page target:

Goal Summary: What will you create?

How does this goal get you closer to your Future Self vision?

What are the first 5 action steps?

1

2

3

4

5

How committed are you to this goal?

① ② ③ ④ ⑤ ⑥ ⑦ ⑧ ⑨ ⑩

Nope "So so" 100%

How do you want to feel during the writing process?

What could get in your way?

How will you create accountability?

- ○ Accountability buddy
- ○ Adding deadlines to my calendar
- ○
- ○

Goal Roadmap

/ / .... Start

/ / .... End

Use this page to create a realistic timeline, milestones & reflection points.

Visual timeline

Note your start & end date for the project. Then, add 2-5 big milestones & dates along the way.

Realistic timeframe

Step 1: Use your calendar to count how many days/weeks you have from start to finish.
Tip: If you count days, work with half days (2-3h block) vs. full days (4-6h block).

.... Available days

Step 2: Deduct holidays, travel, recovery time, or busy weeks from the above number.

.... Realistic days

Bullet-proof the roadmap

Are you confident you can finish this goal on time? If not, which of the following options might help?

- ○ Move the deadline
- ○ Start earlier
- ○ Hire help
- ○ Reduce the scope
- ○ Remove competing tasks
- ○ Delegate parts of this goal
- ○ ....
- ○ ....
- ○ ....

Plan your reflection

I will reflect on my progress and adjust my roadmap on:

/ / .... Date

Goal

Deadline:

Word/Page target:

Goal Summary: What will you create?

How does this goal get you closer to your Future Self vision?

What are the first 5 action steps?

1

2

3

4

5

How committed are you to this goal?

1 2 3 4 5 6 7 8 9 10

Nope "So so" 100%

How do you want to feel during the writing process?

What could get in your way?

How will you create accountability?

- Accountability buddy
- Adding deadlines to my calendar

Goal Roadmap

/ / .... / / ....

Start End

Use this page to create a realistic timeline, milestones & reflection points.

Visual timeline

Note your start & end date for the project. Then, add 2-5 big milestones & dates along the way.

Realistic timeframe

Step 1: Use your calendar to count how many days/weeks you have from start to finish.
Tip: If you count days, work with half days (2-3h block) vs. full days (4-6h block).

.... Available days

Step 2: Deduct holidays, travel, recovery time, or busy weeks from the above number.

.... Realistic days

Bullet-proof the roadmap

Are you confident you can finish this goal on time? If not, which of the following options might help?

- ○ Move the deadline
- ○ Start earlier
- ○ Hire help
- ○ Reduce the scope
- ○ Remove competing tasks
- ○ Delegate parts of this goal
- ○ ....
- ○ ....
- ○ ....

Plan your reflection

I will reflect on my progress and adjust my roadmap on:

/ / .... Date

Goal

Deadline:

Word/Page target:

Goal Summary: What will you create?

How does this goal get you closer to your Future Self vision?

What are the first 5 action steps?

1
2
3
4
5

How committed are you to this goal?

① ② ③ ④ ⑤ ⑥ ⑦ ⑧ ⑨ ⑩

Nope "So so" 100%

How do you want to feel during the writing process?

What could get in your way?

How will you create accountability?

- ○ Accountability buddy
- ○ Adding deadlines to my calendar
- ○
- ○

Goal Roadmap

/ / Start   / / End

Use this page to create a realistic timeline, milestones & reflection points.

Visual timeline

Note your start & end date for the project. Then, add 2-5 big milestones & dates along the way.

Realistic timeframe

Step 1: Use your calendar to count how many days/weeks you have from start to finish.
Tip: If you count days, work with half days (2-3h block) vs. full days (4-6h block).

Available days

Step 2: Deduct holidays, travel, recovery time, or busy weeks from the above number.

Realistic days

Bullet-proof the roadmap

Are you confident you can finish this goal on time? If not, which of the following options might help?

- ○ Move the deadline
- ○ Reduce the scope
- ○
- ○ Start earlier
- ○ Remove competing tasks
- ○
- ○ Hire help
- ○ Delegate parts of this goal
- ○

Plan your reflection

I will reflect on my progress and adjust my roadmap on:

/ / Date

Goal

Deadline:

Word/Page target:

Goal Summary: What will you create?

How does this goal get you closer to your Future Self vision?

What are the first 5 action steps?

1

2

3

4

5

How committed are you to this goal?

① ② ③ ④ ⑤ ⑥ ⑦ ⑧ ⑨ ⑩

Nope "So so" 100%

How do you want to feel during the writing process?

What could get in your way?

How will you create accountability?

- ○ Accountability buddy
- ○ Adding deadlines to my calendar
- ○
- ○

Goal Roadmap

/ / Start

/ / End

Use this page to create a realistic timeline, milestones & reflection points.

Visual timeline

Note your start & end date for the project. Then, add 2-5 big milestones & dates along the way.

Realistic timeframe

Step 1: Use your calendar to count how many days/weeks you have from start to finish.
Tip: If you count days, work with half days (2-3h block) vs. full days (4-6h block).

Available days

Step 2: Deduct holidays, travel, recovery time, or busy weeks from the above number.

Realistic days

Bullet-proof the roadmap

Are you confident you can finish this goal on time? If not, which of the following options might help?

- ○ Move the deadline
- ○ Start earlier
- ○ Hire help
- ○ Reduce the scope
- ○ Remove competing tasks
- ○ Delegate parts of this goal
- ○
- ○
- ○

Plan your reflection

I will reflect on my progress and adjust my roadmap on:

/ / Date

Goal

Deadline:

Word/Page target:

Goal Summary: What will you create?

How does this goal get you closer to your Future Self vision?

What are the first 5 action steps?

1

2

3

4

5

How committed are you to this goal?

1 2 3 4 5 6 7 8 9 10

Nope "So so" 100%

How do you want to feel during the writing process?

What could get in your way?

How will you create accountability?

- Accountability buddy
- Adding deadlines to my calendar

Goal Roadmap

/ / Start

/ / End

Use this page to create a realistic timeline, milestones & reflection points.

Visual timeline

Note your start & end date for the project. Then, add 2-5 big milestones & dates along the way.

Realistic timeframe

Step 1: Use your calendar to count how many days/weeks you have from start to finish.
Tip: If you count days, work with half days (2-3h block) vs. full days (4-6h block).

Available days

Step 2: Deduct holidays, travel, recovery time, or busy weeks from the above number.

Realistic days

Bullet-proof the roadmap

Are you confident you can finish this goal on time? If not, which of the following options might help?

- ○ Move the deadline
- ○ Start earlier
- ○ Hire help
- ○ Reduce the scope
- ○ Remove competing tasks
- ○ Delegate parts of this goal
- ○
- ○
- ○

Plan your reflection

I will reflect on my progress and adjust my roadmap on:

/ / Date

Goal

Deadline:

Word/Page target:

Goal Summary: What will you create?

How does this goal get you closer to your Future Self vision?

What are the first 5 action steps?

1

2

3

4

5

How committed are you to this goal?

① ② ③ ④ ⑤ ⑥ ⑦ ⑧ ⑨ ⑩

Nope "So so" 100%

How do you want to feel during the writing process?

What could get in your way?

How will you create accountability?

- ○ Accountability buddy
- ○ Adding deadlines to my calendar
- ○
- ○

Goal Roadmap

/ / Start

/ / End

Use this page to create a realistic timeline, milestones & reflection points.

Visual timeline

Note your start & end date for the project. Then, add 2-5 big milestones & dates along the way.

Realistic timeframe

Step 1: Use your calendar to count how many days/weeks you have from start to finish.
Tip: If you count days, work with half days (2-3h block) vs. full days (4-6h block).

Available days

Step 2: Deduct holidays, travel, recovery time, or busy weeks from the above number.

Realistic days

Bullet-proof the roadmap

Are you confident you can finish this goal on time? If not, which of the following options might help?

- ○ Move the deadline
- ○ Start earlier
- ○ Hire help
- ○ Reduce the scope
- ○ Remove competing tasks
- ○ Delegate parts of this goal
- ○
- ○
- ○

Plan your reflection

I will reflect on my progress and adjust my roadmap on:

/ / Date

Monthly Focus

Month/Year

Top 3 Priorities

1

2

3

My habit focus this month:

Main activities:

- ○ Plan (outline / read / journal / mind map)
- ○ Draft (new words without stopping)
- ○ Edit (revise / structural edit / proofread)
- ○

MONDAY	TUESDAY	WEDNESDAY	THURSDAY	FRIDAY	SATURDAY	SUNDAY

Monthly Reflection

What are my 3-5 biggest wins from last month?

1.
2.
3.
4.
5.

What worked well?

Where did I get distracted or stuck?

How could this have happened *for* me (not *to* me)? What did I get to learn?

What will I stop / start / continue doing next month?

Stop	Start	Continue

How productive was this month? (1) (2) (3) (4) (5) (6) (7) (8) (9) (10)

Monthly Focus

Month/Year

Top 3 Priorities

1.
2.
3.

My habit focus this month:

Main activities:

- ○ Plan (outline / read / journal / mind map)
- ○ Draft (new words without stopping)
- ○ Edit (revise / structural edit / proofread)
- ○

MONDAY	TUESDAY	WEDNESDAY	THURSDAY	FRIDAY	SATURDAY	SUNDAY

Monthly Reflection

What are my 3-5 biggest wins from last month?

1

2

3

4

5

What worked well?

Where did I get distracted or stuck?

How could this have happened *for* me (not *to* me)? What did I get to learn?

What will I stop / start / continue doing next month?

Stop	Start	Continue

How productive was this month? 1 2 3 4 5 6 7 8 9 10

Monthly Focus

Month/Year

Top 3 Priorities

1

2

3

My habit focus this month:

Main activities:

- ○ Plan (outline / read / journal / mind map)
- ○ Draft (new words without stopping)
- ○ Edit (revise / structural edit / proofread)
- ○

MONDAY	TUESDAY	WEDNESDAY	THURSDAY	FRIDAY	SATURDAY	SUNDAY

Monthly Reflection

What are my 3-5 biggest wins from last month?

1
2
3
4
5

What worked well?

Where did I get distracted or stuck?

How could this have happened *for* me (not *to* me)? What did I get to learn?

What will I stop / start / continue doing next month?

Stop	Start	Continue

How productive was this month? 1 2 3 4 5 6 7 8 9 10

Monthly Focus

Month/Year

Top 3 Priorities

1

2

3

My habit focus this month:

Main activities:

- ○ Plan (outline / read / journal / mind map)
- ○ Draft (new words without stopping)
- ○ Edit (revise / structural edit / proofread)
- ○

MONDAY	TUESDAY	WEDNESDAY	THURSDAY	FRIDAY	SATURDAY	SUNDAY

Monthly Reflection

What are my 3-5 biggest wins from last month?

1.
2.
3.
4.
5.

What worked well?

Where did I get distracted or stuck?

How could this have happened *for* me (not *to* me)? What did I get to learn?

What will I stop / start / continue doing next month?

Stop	Start	Continue

How productive was this month?       7 8 9 10

Monthly Focus

Month/Year

Top 3 Priorities

1

2

3

My habit focus this month:

Main activities:

- ○ Plan (outline / read / journal / mind map)
- ○ Draft (new words without stopping)
- ○ Edit (revise / structural edit / proofread)
- ○

MONDAY	TUESDAY	WEDNESDAY	THURSDAY	FRIDAY	SATURDAY	SUNDAY

Monthly Reflection

What are my 3-5 biggest wins from last month?

1.
2.
3.
4.
5.

What worked well?

Where did I get distracted or stuck?

How could this have happened *for* me (not *to* me)? What did I get to learn?

What will I stop / start / continue doing next month?

Stop	Start	Continue

How productive was this month? (1) (2) (3) (4) (5) (6) (7) (8) (9) (10)

Monthly Focus

Month/Year

Top 3 Priorities

1

2

3

My habit focus this month:

Main activities:

- ○ Plan (outline / read / journal / mind map)
- ○ Draft (new words without stopping)
- ○ Edit (revise / structural edit / proofread)
- ○

MONDAY	TUESDAY	WEDNESDAY	THURSDAY	FRIDAY	SATURDAY	SUNDAY

Monthly Reflection

What are my 3-5 biggest wins from last month?

1.
2.
3.
4.
5.

What worked well?

Where did I get distracted or stuck?

How could this have happened *for* me (not *to* me)? What did I get to learn?

What will I stop / start / continue doing next month?

Stop	Start	Continue

How productive was this month? (1) (2) (3) (4) (5) (6) (7) (8) (9) (10)

Monthly Focus

Month/Year

Top 3 Priorities

1.

2.

3.

My habit focus this month:

Main activities:

- ○ Plan (outline / read / journal / mind map)
- ○ Draft (new words without stopping)
- ○ Edit (revise / structural edit / proofread)
- ○

MONDAY	TUESDAY	WEDNESDAY	THURSDAY	FRIDAY	SATURDAY	SUNDAY

Monthly Reflection

What are my 3-5 biggest wins from last month?

1.
2.
3.
4.
5.

What worked well?

Where did I get distracted or stuck?

How could this have happened *for* me (not *to* me)? What did I get to learn?

What will I stop / start / continue doing next month?

Stop	Start	Continue

How productive was this month? ① ② ③ ④ ⑤ ⑥ ⑦ ⑧ ⑨ ⑩

Monthly Focus

Month/Year

Top 3 Priorities

1.
2.
3.

My habit focus this month:

Main activities:

- ○ Plan (outline / read / journal / mind map)
- ○ Draft (new words without stopping)
- ○ Edit (revise / structural edit / proofread)
- ○

MONDAY	TUESDAY	WEDNESDAY	THURSDAY	FRIDAY	SATURDAY	SUNDAY

Monthly Reflection

What are my 3-5 biggest wins from last month?

1.
2.
3.
4.
5.

What worked well?

Where did I get distracted or stuck?

How could this have happened *for* me (not *to* me)? What did I get to learn?

What will I stop / start / continue doing next month?

Stop	Start	Continue

How productive was this month?      

Monthly Focus

Month/Year

Top 3 Priorities

1

2

3

My habit focus this month:

Main activities:

- ○ Plan (outline / read / journal / mind map)
- ○ Draft (new words without stopping)
- ○ Edit (revise / structural edit / proofread)
- ○

MONDAY	TUESDAY	WEDNESDAY	THURSDAY	FRIDAY	SATURDAY	SUNDAY

Monthly Reflection

What are my 3-5 biggest wins from last month?

1.
2.
3.
4.
5.

What worked well?

Where did I get distracted or stuck?

How could this have happened *for* me (not *to* me)? What did I get to learn?

What will I stop / start / continue doing next month?

Stop	Start	Continue

How productive was this month? ① ② ③ ④ ⑤ ⑥ ⑦ ⑧ ⑨ ⑩

Monthly Focus

Month/Year

Top 3 Priorities

1

2

3

My habit focus this month:

Main activities:

- ○ Plan (outline / read / journal / mind map)
- ○ Draft (new words without stopping)
- ○ Edit (revise / structural edit / proofread)
- ○

MONDAY	TUESDAY	WEDNESDAY	THURSDAY	FRIDAY	SATURDAY	SUNDAY

Monthly Reflection

What are my 3-5 biggest wins from last month?

1
2
3
4
5

What worked well?

Where did I get distracted or stuck?

How could this have happened *for* me (not *to* me)? What did I get to learn?

What will I stop / start / continue doing next month?

Stop	Start	Continue

How productive was this month? 1 2 3 4 5 6 7 8 9 10

Monthly Focus

Month/Year

Top 3 Priorities

1.
2.
3.

My habit focus this month:

Main activities:

- ○ Plan (outline / read / journal / mind map)
- ○ Draft (new words without stopping)
- ○ Edit (revise / structural edit / proofread)
- ○

MONDAY	TUESDAY	WEDNESDAY	THURSDAY	FRIDAY	SATURDAY	SUNDAY

Monthly Reflection

What are my 3-5 biggest wins from last month?

1.
2.
3.
4.
5.

What worked well?

Where did I get distracted or stuck?

How could this have happened *for* me (not *to* me)? What did I get to learn?

What will I stop / start / continue doing next month?

Stop	Start	Continue

How productive was this month? ① ② ③ ④ ⑤ ⑥ ⑦ ⑧ ⑨ ⑩

Monthly Focus

Month/Year

Top 3 Priorities

1

2

3

My habit focus this month:

Main activities:

- ○ Plan (outline / read / journal / mind map)
- ○ Draft (new words without stopping)
- ○ Edit (revise / structural edit / proofread)
- ○

MONDAY	TUESDAY	WEDNESDAY	THURSDAY	FRIDAY	SATURDAY	SUNDAY

Monthly Reflection

What are my 3-5 biggest wins from last month?

1
2
3
4
5

What worked well?

Where did I get distracted or stuck?

How could this have happened *for* me (not *to* me)? What did I get to learn?

What will I stop / start / continue doing next month?

Stop	Start	Continue

How productive was this month? ① ② ③ ④ ⑤ ⑥ ⑦ ⑧ ⑨ ⑩

Weekly Overview

/ /

Week of

My top 3 writing priorities

Goal 1

Goal 2

Goal 3

Break down each goal into smaller steps

Additional tasks, events or deadlines

My habit focus for this week

What I'm taking off my plate...

Reflection: 3 wins or learning points from this week

1

2

3

How productive was this week? 1 2 3 4 5 6 7 8 9 10

Writing Slots

- ○ Top 3 goals
- ○ Plan / draft / edit
- ○ Break times
- ○ Progress (words, hours)

	Monday	Tuesday	Wednesday	Thursday	Friday	Saturday	Sunday
6							
7							
8							
9							
10							
11							
12							
1							
2							
3							
4							
5							
6							
7							
8							
9							
Target							
Actual							

Weekly Overview

/ /

Week of

My top 3 writing priorities

Goal 1	Goal 2	Goal 3

Break down each goal into smaller steps

Additional tasks, events or deadlines

My habit focus for this week

What I'm taking off my plate...

Reflection: 3 wins or learning points from this week

1.
2.
3.

How productive was this week? ① ② ③ ④ ⑤ ⑥ ⑦ ⑧ ⑨ ⑩

Writing Slots

- ○ Top 3 goals
- ○ Plan / draft / edit
- ○ Break times
- ○ Progress (words, hours)

	Monday	Tuesday	Wednesday	Thursday	Friday	Saturday	Sunday
6							
7							
8							
9							
10							
11							
12							
1							
2							
3							
4							
5							
6							
7							
8							
9							
Target							
Actual							

Weekly Overview

/ /
Week of

My top 3 writing priorities

Goal 1

Goal 2

Goal 3

Break down each goal into smaller steps

Additional tasks, events or deadlines

My habit focus for this week

What I'm taking off my plate...

Reflection: 3 wins or learning points from this week

1.
2.
3.

How productive was this week? 1 2 3 4 5 6 7 8 9 10

Writing Slots

- ○ Top 3 goals
- ○ Plan / draft / edit
- ○ Break times
- ○ Progress (words, hours)

	Monday	Tuesday	Wednesday	Thursday	Friday	Saturday	Sunday
6							
7							
8							
9							
10							
11							
12							
1							
2							
3							
4							
5							
6							
7							
8							
9							

Target

Actual

Weekly Overview

/ /
Week of

My top 3 writing priorities

Goal 1	Goal 2	Goal 3

Break down each goal into smaller steps

Additional tasks, events or deadlines

My habit focus for this week

What I'm taking off my plate...

Reflection: 3 wins or learning points from this week

1.
2.
3.

How productive was this week? ① ② ③ ④ ⑤ ⑥ ⑦ ⑧ ⑨ ⑩

Writing Slots

- Top 3 goals
- Plan / draft / edit
- Break times
- Progress (words, hours)

	Monday	Tuesday	Wednesday	Thursday	Friday	Saturday	Sunday
6							
7							
8							
9							
10							
11							
12							
1							
2							
3							
4							
5							
6							
7							
8							
9							
Target							
Actual							

Weekly Overview

/ /

Week of

My top 3 writing priorities

Goal 1	Goal 2	Goal 3

Break down each goal into smaller steps

Additional tasks, events or deadlines

My habit focus for this week

What I'm taking off my plate...

Reflection: 3 wins or learning points from this week

1.
2.
3.

How productive was this week? ① ② ③ ④ ⑤ ⑥ ⑦ ⑧ ⑨ ⑩

Writing Slots

- ○ Top 3 goals
- ○ Plan / draft / edit
- ○ Break times
- ○ Progress (words, hours)

	Monday	Tuesday	Wednesday	Thursday	Friday	Saturday	Sunday
6							
7							
8							
9							
10							
11							
12							
1							
2							
3							
4							
5							
6							
7							
8							
9							
Target							
Actual							

Weekly Overview

/ /
Week of

My top 3 writing priorities

Goal 1	Goal 2	Goal 3

Break down each goal into smaller steps

Additional tasks, events or deadlines

My habit focus for this week

What I'm taking off my plate...

Reflection: 3 wins or learning points from this week

1.
2.
3.

How productive was this week? ① ② ③ ④ ⑤ ⑥ ⑦ ⑧ ⑨ ⑩

Writing Slots

- ○ Top 3 goals
- ○ Plan / draft / edit
- ○ Break times
- ○ Progress (words, hours)

	Monday	Tuesday	Wednesday	Thursday	Friday	Saturday	Sunday
6							
7							
8							
9							
10							
11							
12							
1							
2							
3							
4							
5							
6							
7							
8							
9							
Target							
Actual							

Weekly Overview

Week of / /

My top 3 writing priorities

Goal 1	Goal 2	Goal 3

Break down each goal into smaller steps

Additional tasks, events or deadlines

My habit focus for this week

What I'm taking off my plate...

Reflection: 3 wins or learning points from this week

1.
2.
3.

How productive was this week? ① ② ③ ④ ⑤ ⑥ ⑦ ⑧ ⑨ ⑩

Writing Slots

- ○ Top 3 goals
- ○ Plan / draft / edit
- ○ Break times
- ○ Progress (words, hours)

	Monday	Tuesday	Wednesday	Thursday	Friday	Saturday	Sunday
6							
7							
8							
9							
10							
11							
12							
1							
2							
3							
4							
5							
6							
7							
8							
9							
Target							
Actual							

Weekly Overview

/ /
Week of

My top 3 writing priorities

Goal 1	Goal 2	Goal 3

Break down each goal into smaller steps

Additional tasks, events or deadlines

My habit focus for this week

What I'm taking off my plate...

Reflection: 3 wins or learning points from this week

1.
2.
3.

How productive was this week? ① ② ③ ④ ⑤ ⑥ ⑦ ⑧ ⑨ ⑩

Writing Slots

- ○ Top 3 goals
- ○ Plan / draft / edit
- ○ Break times
- ○ Progress (words, hours)

	Monday	Tuesday	Wednesday	Thursday	Friday	Saturday	Sunday
6							
7							
8							
9							
10							
11							
12							
1							
2							
3							
4							
5							
6							
7							
8							
9							
Target							
Actual							

Weekly Overview

/ /
Week of

My top 3 writing priorities

Goal 1	Goal 2	Goal 3

Break down each goal into smaller steps

Additional tasks, events or deadlines

My habit focus for this week	What I'm taking off my plate...

Reflection: 3 wins or learning points from this week

1.
2.
3.

How productive was this week? ① ② ③ ④ ⑤ ⑥ ⑦ ⑧ ⑨ ⑩

Writing Slots

- ○ Top 3 goals
- ○ Plan / draft / edit
- ○ Break times
- ○ Progress (words, hours)

	Monday	Tuesday	Wednesday	Thursday	Friday	Saturday	Sunday
6							
7							
8							
9							
10							
11							
12							
1							
2							
3							
4							
5							
6							
7							
8							
9							
Target							
Actual							

Weekly Overview

/ /
Week of

My top 3 writing priorities

Goal 1	Goal 2	Goal 3

Break down each goal into smaller steps

Additional tasks, events or deadlines

My habit focus for this week

What I'm taking off my plate...

Reflection: 3 wins or learning points from this week

1.
2.
3.

How productive was this week? ① ② ③ ④ ⑤ ⑥ ⑦ ⑧ ⑨ ⑩

Writing Slots

- ○ Top 3 goals
- ○ Plan / draft / edit
- ○ Break times
- ○ Progress (words, hours)

	Monday	Tuesday	Wednesday	Thursday	Friday	Saturday	Sunday
6							
7							
8							
9							
10							
11							
12							
1							
2							
3							
4							
5							
6							
7							
8							
9							
Target							
Actual							

Weekly Overview

/ /
Week of

My top 3 writing priorities

Goal 1

Goal 2

Goal 3

Break down each goal into smaller steps

Additional tasks, events or deadlines

My habit focus for this week

What I'm taking off my plate...

Reflection: 3 wins or learning points from this week

1.
2.
3.

How productive was this week? ① ② ③ ④ ⑤ ⑥ ⑦ ⑧ ⑨ ⑩

Writing Slots

- ○ Top 3 goals
- ○ Plan / draft / edit
- ○ Break times
- ○ Progress (words, hours)

	Monday	Tuesday	Wednesday	Thursday	Friday	Saturday	Sunday
6							
7							
8							
9							
10							
11							
12							
1							
2							
3							
4							
5							
6							
7							
8							
9							
Target							
Actual							

Weekly Overview

/ /

Week of

My top 3 writing priorities

Goal 1	Goal 2	Goal 3

Break down each goal into smaller steps

Additional tasks, events or deadlines

My habit focus for this week

What I'm taking off my plate...

Reflection: 3 wins or learning points from this week

1.
2.
3.

How productive was this week? ① ② ③ ④ ⑤ ⑥ ⑦ ⑧ ⑨ ⑩

Writing Slots

- ○ Top 3 goals
- ○ Plan / draft / edit
- ○ Break times
- ○ Progress (words, hours)

	Monday	Tuesday	Wednesday	Thursday	Friday	Saturday	Sunday
6							
7							
8							
9							
10							
11							
12							
1							
2							
3							
4							
5							
6							
7							
8							
9							
Target							
Actual							

Weekly Overview

Week of

My top 3 writing priorities

Goal 1

Goal 2

Goal 3

Break down each goal into smaller steps

Additional tasks, events or deadlines

My habit focus for this week

What I'm taking off my plate...

Reflection: 3 wins or learning points from this week

1.
2.
3.

How productive was this week? ① ② ③ ④ ⑤ ⑥ ⑦ ⑧ ⑨ ⑩

Writing Slots

- ○ Top 3 goals
- ○ Plan / draft / edit
- ○ Break times
- ○ Progress (words, hours)

	Monday	Tuesday	Wednesday	Thursday	Friday	Saturday	Sunday
6							
7							
8							
9							
10							
11							
12							
1							
2							
3							
4							
5							
6							
7							
8							
9							
Target							
Actual							

Weekly Overview

/ /

Week of

My top 3 writing priorities

Goal 1	Goal 2	Goal 3

Break down each goal into smaller steps

Additional tasks, events or deadlines

My habit focus for this week

What I'm taking off my plate...

Reflection: 3 wins or learning points from this week

1

2

3

How productive was this week? 1 2 3 4 5 6 7 8 9 10

Writing Slots

- Top 3 goals
- Plan / draft / edit
- Break times
- Progress (words, hours)

	Monday	Tuesday	Wednesday	Thursday	Friday	Saturday	Sunday
6							
7							
8							
9							
10							
11							
12							
1							
2							
3							
4							
5							
6							
7							
8							
9							
Target							
Actual							

Weekly Overview

/ /
Week of

My top 3 writing priorities

Goal 1

Goal 2

Goal 3

Break down each goal into smaller steps

Additional tasks, events or deadlines

My habit focus for this week

What I'm taking off my plate...

Reflection: 3 wins or learning points from this week

①

②

③

How productive was this week? ① ② ③ ④ ⑤ ⑥ ⑦ ⑧ ⑨ ⑩

Writing Slots

- ○ Top 3 goals
- ○ Plan / draft / edit
- ○ Break times
- ○ Progress (words, hours)

	Monday	Tuesday	Wednesday	Thursday	Friday	Saturday	Sunday
6							
7							
8							
9							
10							
11							
12							
1							
2							
3							
4							
5							
6							
7							
8							
9							
Target							
Actual							

Weekly Overview

/ /
Week of

My top 3 writing priorities

Goal 1	Goal 2	Goal 3

Break down each goal into smaller steps

Additional tasks, events or deadlines

My habit focus for this week

What I'm taking off my plate...

Reflection: 3 wins or learning points from this week

1.
2.
3.

How productive was this week? ① ② ③ ④ ⑤ ⑥ ⑦ ⑧ ⑨ ⑩

Writing Slots

○ Top 3 goals
○ Plan / draft / edit
○ Break times
○ Progress (words, hours)

	Monday	Tuesday	Wednesday	Thursday	Friday	Saturday	Sunday
6							
7							
8							
9							
10							
11							
12							
1							
2							
3							
4							
5							
6							
7							
8							
9							
Target							
Actual							

Weekly Overview

/ /
Week of

My top 3 writing priorities

Goal 1	Goal 2	Goal 3

Break down each goal into smaller steps

Additional tasks, events or deadlines

My habit focus for this week

What I'm taking off my plate...

Reflection: 3 wins or learning points from this week

1
2
3

How productive was this week? 1 2 3 4 5 6 7 8 9 10

Writing Slots

- ○ Top 3 goals
- ○ Plan / draft / edit
- ○ Break times
- ○ Progress (words, hours)

	Monday	Tuesday	Wednesday	Thursday	Friday	Saturday	Sunday
6							
7							
8							
9							
10							
11							
12							
1							
2							
3							
4							
5							
6							
7							
8							
9							
Target							
Actual							

Weekly Overview

/ /

Week of

My top 3 writing priorities

Goal 1	Goal 2	Goal 3

Break down each goal into smaller steps

Additional tasks, events or deadlines

My habit focus for this week

What I'm taking off my plate...

Reflection: 3 wins or learning points from this week

1.
2.
3.

How productive was this week? ① ② ③ ④ ⑤ ⑥ ⑦ ⑧ ⑨ ⑩

Writing Slots

- ○ Top 3 goals
- ○ Plan / draft / edit
- ○ Break times
- ○ Progress (words, hours)

	Monday	Tuesday	Wednesday	Thursday	Friday	Saturday	Sunday
6							
7							
8							
9							
10							
11							
12							
1							
2							
3							
4							
5							
6							
7							
8							
9							
Target							
Actual							

Weekly Overview

Week of

My top 3 writing priorities

Goal 1

Goal 2

Goal 3

Break down each goal into smaller steps

Additional tasks, events or deadlines

My habit focus for this week

What I'm taking off my plate...

Reflection: 3 wins or learning points from this week

1.
2.
3.

How productive was this week? 1 2 3 4 5 6 7 8 9 10

Writing Slots

- ○ Top 3 goals
- ○ Plan / draft / edit
- ○ Break times
- ○ Progress (words, hours)

	Monday	Tuesday	Wednesday	Thursday	Friday	Saturday	Sunday
6							
7							
8							
9							
10							
11							
12							
1							
2							
3							
4							
5							
6							
7							
8							
9							
Target							
Actual							

Weekly Overview

Week of

My top 3 writing priorities

Goal 1

Goal 2

Goal 3

Break down each goal into smaller steps

Additional tasks, events or deadlines

My habit focus for this week

What I'm taking off my plate...

Reflection: 3 wins or learning points from this week

1
2
3

How productive was this week? 1 2 3 4 5 6 7 8 9 10

Writing Slots

- ○ Top 3 goals
- ○ Plan / draft / edit
- ○ Break times
- ○ Progress (words, hours)

	Monday	Tuesday	Wednesday	Thursday	Friday	Saturday	Sunday
6							
7							
8							
9							
10							
11							
12							
1							
2							
3							
4							
5							
6							
7							
8							
9							
Target							
Actual							

Weekly Overview

/ /
Week of

My top 3 writing priorities

Goal 1	Goal 2	Goal 3

Break down each goal into smaller steps

Additional tasks, events or deadlines

My habit focus for this week

What I'm taking off my plate...

Reflection: 3 wins or learning points from this week

(1)

(2)

(3)

How productive was this week? (1) (2) (3) (4) (5) (6) (7) (8) (9) (10)

Writing Slots

- ○ Top 3 goals
- ○ Plan / draft / edit
- ○ Break times
- ○ Progress (words, hours)

	Monday	Tuesday	Wednesday	Thursday	Friday	Saturday	Sunday
6							
7							
8							
9							
10							
11							
12							
1							
2							
3							
4							
5							
6							
7							
8							
9							
Target							
Actual							

Weekly Overview

Week of

My top 3 writing priorities

Goal 1	Goal 2	Goal 3

Break down each goal into smaller steps

Additional tasks, events or deadlines

My habit focus for this week

What I'm taking off my plate...

Reflection: 3 wins or learning points from this week

1.
2.
3.

How productive was this week? ① ② ③ ④ ⑤ ⑥ ⑦ ⑧ ⑨ ⑩

Writing Slots

- ○ Top 3 goals
- ○ Break times
- ○ Plan / draft / edit
- ○ Progress (words, hours)

	Monday	Tuesday	Wednesday	Thursday	Friday	Saturday	Sunday
6							
7							
8							
9							
10							
11							
12							
1							
2							
3							
4							
5							
6							
7							
8							
9							
Target							
Actual							

Weekly Overview

/ /
Week of

My top 3 writing priorities

Goal 1	Goal 2	Goal 3

Break down each goal into smaller steps

Additional tasks, events or deadlines

My habit focus for this week

What I'm taking off my plate...

Reflection: 3 wins or learning points from this week

1.
2.
3.

How productive was this week? ① ② ③ ④ ⑤ ⑥ ⑦ ⑧ ⑨ ⑩

Writing Slots

- ○ Top 3 goals
- ○ Plan / draft / edit
- ○ Break times
- ○ Progress (words, hours)

	Monday	Tuesday	Wednesday	Thursday	Friday	Saturday	Sunday
6							
7							
8							
9							
10							
11							
12							
1							
2							
3							
4							
5							
6							
7							
8							
9							
Target							
Actual							

Weekly Overview

/ /
Week of

My top 3 writing priorities

Goal 1	Goal 2	Goal 3

Break down each goal into smaller steps

Additional tasks, events or deadlines

My habit focus for this week

What I'm taking off my plate...

Reflection: 3 wins or learning points from this week

1.
2.
3.

How productive was this week? ① ② ③ ④ ⑤ ⑥ ⑦ ⑧ ⑨ ⑩

Writing Slots

- ○ Top 3 goals
- ○ Plan / draft / edit
- ○ Break times
- ○ Progress (words, hours)

	Monday	Tuesday	Wednesday	Thursday	Friday	Saturday	Sunday
6							
7							
8							
9							
10							
11							
12							
1							
2							
3							
4							
5							
6							
7							
8							
9							
Target							
Actual							

Weekly Overview

/ /
Week of

My top 3 writing priorities

Goal 1	Goal 2	Goal 3

Break down each goal into smaller steps

Additional tasks, events or deadlines

My habit focus for this week

What I'm taking off my plate...

Reflection: 3 wins or learning points from this week

1.
2.
3.

How productive was this week? ① ② ③ ④ ⑤ ⑥ ⑦ ⑧ ⑨ ⑩

Writing Slots

- ○ Top 3 goals
- ○ Plan / draft / edit
- ○ Break times
- ○ Progress (words, hours)

	Monday	Tuesday	Wednesday	Thursday	Friday	Saturday	Sunday
6							
7							
8							
9							
10							
11							
12							
1							
2							
3							
4							
5							
6							
7							
8							
9							
Target							
Actual							

Weekly Overview

/ /
Week of

My top 3 writing priorities

Goal 1

Goal 2

Goal 3

Break down each goal into smaller steps

Additional tasks, events or deadlines

My habit focus for this week

What I'm taking off my plate...

Reflection: 3 wins or learning points from this week

①
②
③

How productive was this week? ① ② ③ ④ ⑤ ⑥ ⑦ ⑧ ⑨ ⑩

Writing Slots

- ○ Top 3 goals
- ○ Break times
- ○ Plan / draft / edit
- ○ Progress (words, hours)

	Monday	Tuesday	Wednesday	Thursday	Friday	Saturday	Sunday
6							
7							
8							
9							
10							
11							
12							
1							
2							
3							
4							
5							
6							
7							
8							
9							
Target							
Actual							

Weekly Overview

/ /
Week of

My top 3 writing priorities

Goal 1	Goal 2	Goal 3

Break down each goal into smaller steps

Additional tasks, events or deadlines

My habit focus for this week	What I'm taking off my plate...

Reflection: 3 wins or learning points from this week

1.
2.
3.

How productive was this week? ① ② ③ ④ ⑤ ⑥ ⑦ ⑧ ⑨ ⑩

Writing Slots

- ○ Top 3 goals
- ○ Plan / draft / edit
- ○ Break times
- ○ Progress (words, hours)

	Monday	Tuesday	Wednesday	Thursday	Friday	Saturday	Sunday
6							
7							
8							
9							
10							
11							
12							
1							
2							
3							
4							
5							
6							
7							
8							
9							
Target							
Actual							

Weekly Overview

/ /
Week of

My top 3 writing priorities

Goal 1	Goal 2	Goal 3

Break down each goal into smaller steps

Additional tasks, events or deadlines

My habit focus for this week

What I'm taking off my plate...

Reflection: 3 wins or learning points from this week

1.
2.
3.

How productive was this week? ① ② ③ ④ ⑤ ⑥ ⑦ ⑧ ⑨ ⑩

Writing Slots

○ Top 3 goals
○ Plan / draft / edit
○ Break times
○ Progress (words, hours)

	Monday	Tuesday	Wednesday	Thursday	Friday	Saturday	Sunday
6							
7							
8							
9							
10							
11							
12							
1							
2							
3							
4							
5							
6							
7							
8							
9							
Target							
Actual							

Weekly Overview

/ /
Week of

My top 3 writing priorities

Goal 1

Goal 2

Goal 3

Break down each goal into smaller steps

Additional tasks, events or deadlines

My habit focus for this week

What I'm taking off my plate...

Reflection: 3 wins or learning points from this week

①

②

③

How productive was this week? ① ② ③ ④ ⑤ ⑥ ⑦ ⑧ ⑨ ⑩

Writing Slots

- ○ Top 3 goals
- ○ Plan / draft / edit
- ○ Break times
- ○ Progress (words, hours)

	Monday	Tuesday	Wednesday	Thursday	Friday	Saturday	Sunday
6							
7							
8							
9							
10							
11							
12							
1							
2							
3							
4							
5							
6							
7							
8							
9							
Target							
Actual							

Weekly Overview

/ /

Week of

My top 3 writing priorities

Goal 1	Goal 2	Goal 3

Break down each goal into smaller steps

Additional tasks, events or deadlines

My habit focus for this week

What I'm taking off my plate...

Reflection: 3 wins or learning points from this week

1.
2.
3.

How productive was this week? ① ② ③ ④ ⑤ ⑥ ⑦ ⑧ ⑨ ⑩

Writing Slots

- ○ Top 3 goals
- ○ Plan / draft / edit
- ○ Break times
- ○ Progress (words, hours)

	Monday	Tuesday	Wednesday	Thursday	Friday	Saturday	Sunday
6							
7							
8							
9							
10							
11							
12							
1							
2							
3							
4							
5							
6							
7							
8							
9							
Target							
Actual							

Weekly Overview

/ /
Week of

My top 3 writing priorities

Goal 1	Goal 2	Goal 3

Break down each goal into smaller steps

Additional tasks, events or deadlines

My habit focus for this week

What I'm taking off my plate...

Reflection: 3 wins or learning points from this week

1.
2.
3.

How productive was this week? ① ② ③ ④ ⑤ ⑥ ⑦ ⑧ ⑨ ⑩

Writing Slots

- ○ Top 3 goals
- ○ Plan / draft / edit
- ○ Break times
- ○ Progress (words, hours)

	Monday	Tuesday	Wednesday	Thursday	Friday	Saturday	Sunday
6							
7							
8							
9							
10							
11							
12							
1							
2							
3							
4							
5							
6							
7							
8							
9							
Target							
Actual							

Weekly Overview

/ /
Week of

My top 3 writing priorities

Goal 1	Goal 2	Goal 3

Break down each goal into smaller steps

Additional tasks, events or deadlines

My habit focus for this week

What I'm taking off my plate...

Reflection: 3 wins or learning points from this week

1.
2.
3.

How productive was this week? ① ② ③ ④ ⑤ ⑥ ⑦ ⑧ ⑨ ⑩

Writing Slots

- ○ Top 3 goals
- ○ Plan / draft / edit
- ○ Break times
- ○ Progress (words, hours)

	Monday	Tuesday	Wednesday	Thursday	Friday	Saturday	Sunday
6							
7							
8							
9							
10							
11							
12							
1							
2							
3							
4							
5							
6							
7							
8							
9							
Target							
Actual							

Weekly Overview

/ /
Week of

My top 3 writing priorities

Goal 1	Goal 2	Goal 3

Break down each goal into smaller steps

Additional tasks, events or deadlines

My habit focus for this week

What I'm taking off my plate...

Reflection: 3 wins or learning points from this week

1.
2.
3.

How productive was this week? ① ② ③ ④ ⑤ ⑥ ⑦ ⑧ ⑨ ⑩

Writing Slots

- ○ Top 3 goals
- ○ Plan / draft / edit
- ○ Break times
- ○ Progress (words, hours)

	Monday	Tuesday	Wednesday	Thursday	Friday	Saturday	Sunday
6							
7							
8							
9							
10							
11							
12							
1							
2							
3							
4							
5							
6							
7							
8							
9							
Target							
Actual							

Weekly Overview

/ /
Week of

My top 3 writing priorities

Goal 1

Goal 2

Goal 3

Break down each goal into smaller steps

Additional tasks, events or deadlines

My habit focus for this week

What I'm taking off my plate...

Reflection: 3 wins or learning points from this week

1

2

3

How productive was this week? 1 2 3 4 5 6 7 8 9 10

Writing Slots

- ○ Top 3 goals
- ○ Plan / draft / edit
- ○ Break times
- ○ Progress (words, hours)

	Monday	Tuesday	Wednesday	Thursday	Friday	Saturday	Sunday
6							
7							
8							
9							
10							
11							
12							
1							
2							
3							
4							
5							
6							
7							
8							
9							
Target							
Actual							

Weekly Overview

/ /

Week of

My top 3 writing priorities

Goal 1	Goal 2	Goal 3

Break down each goal into smaller steps

Additional tasks, events or deadlines

My habit focus for this week	What I'm taking off my plate...

Reflection: 3 wins or learning points from this week

1.
2.
3.

How productive was this week? ① ② ③ ④ ⑤ ⑥ ⑦ ⑧ ⑨ ⑩

Writing Slots

- ○ Top 3 goals
- ○ Plan / draft / edit
- ○ Break times
- ○ Progress (words, hours)

	Monday	Tuesday	Wednesday	Thursday	Friday	Saturday	Sunday
6							
7							
8							
9							
10							
11							
12							
1							
2							
3							
4							
5							
6							
7							
8							
9							
Target							
Actual							

Weekly Overview

/ /
Week of

My top 3 writing priorities

Goal 1

Goal 2

Goal 3

Break down each goal into smaller steps

Additional tasks, events or deadlines

My habit focus for this week

What I'm taking off my plate...

Reflection: 3 wins or learning points from this week

1
2
3

How productive was this week? 1 2 3 4 5 6 7 8 9 10

Writing Slots

- ○ Top 3 goals
- ○ Break times
- ○ Plan / draft / edit
- ○ Progress (words, hours)

	Monday	Tuesday	Wednesday	Thursday	Friday	Saturday	Sunday
6							
7							
8							
9							
10							
11							
12							
1							
2							
3							
4							
5							
6							
7							
8							
9							
Target							
Actual							

Weekly Overview

/ /
Week of

My top 3 writing priorities

Goal 1	Goal 2	Goal 3

Break down each goal into smaller steps

Additional tasks, events or deadlines

My habit focus for this week

What I'm taking off my plate...

Reflection: 3 wins or learning points from this week

1.
2.
3.

How productive was this week? ① ② ③ ④ ⑤ ⑥ ⑦ ⑧ ⑨ ⑩

Writing Slots

- ○ Top 3 goals
- ○ Plan / draft / edit
- ○ Break times
- ○ Progress (words, hours)

	Monday	Tuesday	Wednesday	Thursday	Friday	Saturday	Sunday
6							
7							
8							
9							
10							
11							
12							
1							
2							
3							
4							
5							
6							
7							
8							
9							
Target							
Actual							

Weekly Overview

/ /
Week of

My top 3 writing priorities

Goal 1	Goal 2	Goal 3

Break down each goal into smaller steps

Additional tasks, events or deadlines

My habit focus for this week

What I'm taking off my plate...

Reflection: 3 wins or learning points from this week

1.
2.
3.

How productive was this week? ① ② ③ ④ ⑤ ⑥ ⑦ ⑧ ⑨ ⑩

Writing Slots

- ○ Top 3 goals
- ○ Plan / draft / edit
- ○ Break times
- ○ Progress (words, hours)

	Monday	Tuesday	Wednesday	Thursday	Friday	Saturday	Sunday
6							
7							
8							
9							
10							
11							
12							
1							
2							
3							
4							
5							
6							
7							
8							
9							
Target							
Actual							

Weekly Overview

/ /

Week of

My top 3 writing priorities

Goal 1	Goal 2	Goal 3

Break down each goal into smaller steps

Additional tasks, events or deadlines

My habit focus for this week

What I'm taking off my plate...

Reflection: 3 wins or learning points from this week

1.
2.
3.

How productive was this week? ① ② ③ ④ ⑤ ⑥ ⑦ ⑧ ⑨ ⑩

Writing Slots

- ○ Top 3 goals
- ○ Plan / draft / edit
- ○ Break times
- ○ Progress (words, hours)

	Monday	Tuesday	Wednesday	Thursday	Friday	Saturday	Sunday
6							
7							
8							
9							
10							
11							
12							
1							
2							
3							
4							
5							
6							
7							
8							
9							
Target							
Actual							

Weekly Overview

/ /

Week of

My top 3 writing priorities

Goal 1	Goal 2	Goal 3

Break down each goal into smaller steps

Additional tasks, events or deadlines

My habit focus for this week

What I'm taking off my plate...

Reflection: 3 wins or learning points from this week

1.
2.
3.

How productive was this week? ① ② ③ ④ ⑤ ⑥ ⑦ ⑧ ⑨ ⑩

Writing Slots

- ○ Top 3 goals
- ○ Plan / draft / edit
- ○ Break times
- ○ Progress (words, hours)

	Monday	Tuesday	Wednesday	Thursday	Friday	Saturday	Sunday
6							
7							
8							
9							
10							
11							
12							
1							
2							
3							
4							
5							
6							
7							
8							
9							

Target

Actual

Weekly Overview

/ /
Week of

My top 3 writing priorities

Goal 1	Goal 2	Goal 3

Break down each goal into smaller steps

Additional tasks, events or deadlines

My habit focus for this week

What I'm taking off my plate...

Reflection: 3 wins or learning points from this week

1.
2.
3.

How productive was this week? ① ② ③ ④ ⑤ ⑥ ⑦ ⑧ ⑨ ⑩

Writing Slots

- ○ Top 3 goals
- ○ Plan / draft / edit
- ○ Break times
- ○ Progress (words, hours)

	Monday	Tuesday	Wednesday	Thursday	Friday	Saturday	Sunday
6							
7							
8							
9							
10							
11							
12							
1							
2							
3							
4							
5							
6							
7							
8							
9							
Target							
Actual							

Weekly Overview

/ /
Week of

My top 3 writing priorities

Goal 1

Goal 2

Goal 3

Break down each goal into smaller steps

Additional tasks, events or deadlines

My habit focus for this week

What I'm taking off my plate...

Reflection: 3 wins or learning points from this week

①
②
③

How productive was this week? ① ② ③ ④ ⑤ ⑥ ⑦ ⑧ ⑨ ⑩

Writing Slots

- ○ Top 3 goals
- ○ Plan / draft / edit
- ○ Break times
- ○ Progress (words, hours)

	Monday	Tuesday	Wednesday	Thursday	Friday	Saturday	Sunday
6							
7							
8							
9							
10							
11							
12							
1							
2							
3							
4							
5							
6							
7							
8							
9							
Target							
Actual							

Weekly Overview

/ /

Week of

My top 3 writing priorities

Goal 1	Goal 2	Goal 3

Break down each goal into smaller steps

Additional tasks, events or deadlines

My habit focus for this week

What I'm taking off my plate...

Reflection: 3 wins or learning points from this week

1.
2.
3.

How productive was this week? 1 2 3 4 5 6 7 8 9 10

Writing Slots

- ○ Top 3 goals
- ○ Plan / draft / edit
- ○ Break times
- ○ Progress (words, hours)

	Monday	Tuesday	Wednesday	Thursday	Friday	Saturday	Sunday
6							
7							
8							
9							
10							
11							
12							
1							
2							
3							
4							
5							
6							
7							
8							
9							
Target							
Actual							

Weekly Overview

/ /
Week of

My top 3 writing priorities

Goal 1	Goal 2	Goal 3

Break down each goal into smaller steps

Additional tasks, events or deadlines

My habit focus for this week

What I'm taking off my plate...

Reflection: 3 wins or learning points from this week

①
②
③

How productive was this week? ① ② ③ ④ ⑤ ⑥ ⑦ ⑧ ⑨ ⑩

Writing Slots

- ○ Top 3 goals
- ○ Plan / draft / edit
- ○ Break times
- ○ Progress (words, hours)

	Monday	Tuesday	Wednesday	Thursday	Friday	Saturday	Sunday
6							
7							
8							
9							
10							
11							
12							
1							
2							
3							
4							
5							
6							
7							
8							
9							
Target							
Actual							

Weekly Overview

/ /
Week of

My top 3 writing priorities

Goal 1

Goal 2

Goal 3

Break down each goal into smaller steps

Additional tasks, events or deadlines

My habit focus for this week

What I'm taking off my plate...

Reflection: 3 wins or learning points from this week

1

2

3

How productive was this week? 1 2 3 4 5 6 7 8 9 10

Writing Slots

- ○ Top 3 goals
- ○ Plan / draft / edit
- ○ Break times
- ○ Progress (words, hours)

	Monday	Tuesday	Wednesday	Thursday	Friday	Saturday	Sunday
6							
7							
8							
9							
10							
11							
12							
1							
2							
3							
4							
5							
6							
7							
8							
9							
Target							
Actual							

Weekly Overview

/ /
Week of

My top 3 writing priorities

Goal 1

Goal 2

Goal 3

Break down each goal into smaller steps

Additional tasks, events or deadlines

My habit focus for this week

What I'm taking off my plate...

Reflection: 3 wins or learning points from this week

1

2

3

How productive was this week? 1 2 3 4 5 6 7 8 9 10

Writing Slots

- ○ Top 3 goals
- ○ Plan / draft / edit
- ○ Break times
- ○ Progress (words, hours)

	Monday	Tuesday	Wednesday	Thursday	Friday	Saturday	Sunday
6							
7							
8							
9							
10							
11							
12							
1							
2							
3							
4							
5							
6							
7							
8							
9							
Target							
Actual							

Weekly Overview

/ /
Week of

My top 3 writing priorities

Goal 1

Goal 2

Goal 3

Break down each goal into smaller steps

Additional tasks, events or deadlines

My habit focus for this week

What I'm taking off my plate...

Reflection: 3 wins or learning points from this week

1.
2.
3.

How productive was this week? (1) (2) (3) (4) (5) (6) (7) (8) (9) (10)

Writing Slots

- ○ Top 3 goals
- ○ Plan / draft / edit
- ○ Break times
- ○ Progress (words, hours)

	Monday	Tuesday	Wednesday	Thursday	Friday	Saturday	Sunday
6							
7							
8							
9							
10							
11							
12							
1							
2							
3							
4							
5							
6							
7							
8							
9							
Target							
Actual							

Weekly Overview

Week of / /

My top 3 writing priorities

Goal 1	Goal 2	Goal 3

Break down each goal into smaller steps

Additional tasks, events or deadlines

My habit focus for this week

What I'm taking off my plate...

Reflection: 3 wins or learning points from this week

1.
2.
3.

How productive was this week? ① ② ③ ④ ⑤ ⑥ ⑦ ⑧ ⑨ ⑩

Writing Slots

- ○ Top 3 goals
- ○ Plan / draft / edit
- ○ Break times
- ○ Progress (words, hours)

	Monday	Tuesday	Wednesday	Thursday	Friday	Saturday	Sunday
6							
7							
8							
9							
10							
11							
12							
1							
2							
3							
4							
5							
6							
7							
8							
9							
Target							
Actual							

Weekly Overview

/ /
Week of

My top 3 writing priorities

Goal 1	Goal 2	Goal 3

Break down each goal into smaller steps

Additional tasks, events or deadlines

My habit focus for this week

What I'm taking off my plate...

Reflection: 3 wins or learning points from this week

1.
2.
3.

How productive was this week? ① ② ③ ④ ⑤ ⑥ ⑦ ⑧ ⑨ ⑩

Writing Slots

- ○ Top 3 goals
- ○ Plan / draft / edit
- ○ Break times
- ○ Progress (words, hours)

	Monday	Tuesday	Wednesday	Thursday	Friday	Saturday	Sunday
6							
7							
8							
9							
10							
11							
12							
1							
2							
3							
4							
5							
6							
7							
8							
9							
Target							
Actual							

Weekly Overview

/ /
Week of

My top 3 writing priorities

Goal 1

Goal 2

Goal 3

Break down each goal into smaller steps

Additional tasks, events or deadlines

My habit focus for this week

What I'm taking off my plate...

Reflection: 3 wins or learning points from this week

①

②

③

How productive was this week? ① ② ③ ④ ⑤ ⑥ ⑦ ⑧ ⑨ ⑩

Writing Slots

- ○ Top 3 goals
- ○ Break times
- ○ Plan / draft / edit
- ○ Progress (words, hours)

	Monday	Tuesday	Wednesday	Thursday	Friday	Saturday	Sunday
6							
7							
8							
9							
10							
11							
12							
1							
2							
3							
4							
5							
6							
7							
8							
9							
Target							
Actual							

Weekly Overview

/ /

Week of

My top 3 writing priorities

Goal 1	Goal 2	Goal 3

Break down each goal into smaller steps

Additional tasks, events or deadlines

My habit focus for this week

What I'm taking off my plate...

Reflection: 3 wins or learning points from this week

1.
2.
3.

How productive was this week? (1) (2) (3) (4) (5) (6) (7) (8) (9) (10)

Writing Slots

- ○ Top 3 goals
- ○ Plan / draft / edit
- ○ Break times
- ○ Progress (words, hours)

	Monday	Tuesday	Wednesday	Thursday	Friday	Saturday	Sunday
6							
7							
8							
9							
10							
11							
12							
1							
2							
3							
4							
5							
6							
7							
8							
9							
Target							
Actual							

Weekly Overview

/ /
Week of

My top 3 writing priorities

Goal 1	Goal 2	Goal 3

Break down each goal into smaller steps

Additional tasks, events or deadlines

My habit focus for this week

What I'm taking off my plate...

Reflection: 3 wins or learning points from this week

1.
2.
3.

How productive was this week? ① ② ③ ④ ⑤ ⑥ ⑦ ⑧ ⑨ ⑩

Writing Slots

- ○ Top 3 goals
- ○ Break times
- ○ Plan / draft / edit
- ○ Progress (words, hours)

	Monday	Tuesday	Wednesday	Thursday	Friday	Saturday	Sunday
6							
7							
8							
9							
10							
11							
12							
1							
2							
3							
4							
5							
6							
7							
8							
9							
Target							
Actual							

Congratulations!

You have completed your 52 weeks of writing!

Let's celebrate this moment! You have learned to set better goals, optimise your flow, and establish a regular writing habit.

Let's keep going and prepare for the next 12 months so that you continue to focus and make progress on your writing goals.

Sign ____________________

Date finished ____________________

Your Writer's Toolbox

In the next section, you will find the best tools to help you write even faster and easier.

"Your Habit Vision"	Identify your desired habits
"Your Flow Ritual"	Learn a simple flow ritual and apply it immediately
"Mindsweep & Goal Filter"	When you're overwhelmed with too many goals, use this!

If you're stuck, here are 2 simple tools that can help you unblock yourself:

"Your Writer's Block"	When you're completely blocked, identify deeper issues & find solutions
"10-Minute Backup List"	Use small pockets of time even on busy days

List any additional resources you have found helpful:

....

....

....

....

....

....

....

Find tips, training & planning tools at

THEWRITEHABITPLANNER.COM/GETSTARTED

Your Habit Vision

If you could establish 3 habits that help you write regularly, what would they be?

-
-
-

Which people, courses or communities could help you apply these habits?

Let's envision your ideal Future Self schedule. What would a productive writing day - and day off - look like? And could you tweak one small thing in your *current* schedule to get closer to your vision?

Ideal working day	Ideal day off
7 am	7 am
8 am	8 am
9 am	9 am
10 am	10 am
11 am	11 am
12 am	12 am
1 pm	1 pm
2 pm	2 pm
3 pm	3 pm
4 pm	4 pm
5 pm	5 pm
7 pm	7 pm
8 pm	8 pm
9 pm	9 pm

Your Flow Ritual

What helps your BODY to let go and enter a flow state? List 3-5 things (e.g. take a breath, movement)

What helps your MIND to focus? List 3-5 things (e.g. phone off, write down goals)

Based on the above, pick three items and stack them together to build your personal Flow Ritual. Use this ritual for 7 days at least - each time before you start writing (e.g. take 3 breaths > phone off > set goals).

1

2

3

"Flow is when disciplines and deadlines have become obsolete."
- Dr Nicole Janz

Your Mindsweep

Date

Use this tool whenever your to-do list feels cluttered - or at the start of each quarter, month, week.

Your top three priorities

All the other tasks on your list

Mark each goal's value for your Future Self in the column on the right.

* = Hell, yes! This gets me to my Future Self!

L = Lesser goal. I'll drop / delay / delegate it.

? = Unsure. I'll fill in the goal filter.

Your Goal Filter

Date

Use this tool when you're unsure if you should drop a goal (but you secretly want to).

Goal summary

Deadline

What are your key motivations to complete this goal? (rank them)

Is this goal the best use of your time right now?

Clearly not! ① ② ③ ④ ⑤ ⑥ ⑦ ⑧ ⑨ ⑩ Absolutely yes!

What's the worst that could happen if you said no?

What would you do with the time freed up if you removed the goal?

Decision:

- Hell, yes!
- No (delegate / delay / drop)

You'll communicate your decision & remove the goal from your list on:

Your Writer's Block

Which project are you blocked with? What stage is it in and where are you stuck?

How bad does it feel in this moment?

Where can you feel the block in your body? Scan it from top to bottom and write down where tension, pain, or other sensations appear. Lay your hand gently on that area, and take three breaths.

If you could take a guess at what your creative block is trying to tell you, what might that be? Which valuable insights arise?

"Feel the fear... and write anyway. Write through uncertainty, write towards clarity, and write yourself out of block."

— Dr Nicole Janz

"Every moment of creative block presents an opportunity. It's your chance to heal, reconnect, and recommit to your project."
— Dr Nicole Janz

Which of the below "12 ways out of block" could help you?

- [ ] I need to take a break and recover.
- [ ] I need to do more research before I can write.
- [ ] I need to allow myself to write a really bad, shitty first draft.
- [ ] I need to drop or delegate this project to work on my real priority.
- [ ] I need to adjust my flow ritual to get into deep work again.
- [ ] I need to re-set my roadmap and deadlines and start fresh.
- [ ] I need to find someone to hold me accountable.
- [ ] I need to make this project "good enough" but not perfect.
- [ ] I need to drop something from my schedule to prioritise this project.
- [ ] I need to journal on why this project helps be become my Future Self.
- [ ] I need to start writing in tiny steps, even just 10 minutes a day.
- [ ] I need to talk to a coach / editor / friend to clarify what's going on.

If your Future Self was sitting in the room with you right now, what advice would they give you?

What's one tiny, manageable step you're going to take?

10-Minute Backup List

You can 'be a writer' even on busy days - with the 10-Minute Rule. For each project, make a list of preparation, writing & editing tasks are small and can be done anywhere (even just in your head!).

10-min PREPARATION tasks:

10-min DRAFTING tasks:

10-min EDITING tasks:

"10 minutes is all it takes to feel like a writer every single day."
- Dr Nicole Janz

Your Free Course

The Write Habit is not just a planner - it's a productivity system.

And it comes with a FREE TRAINING COURSE!

Just for you, there's an entire library of tutorials, trainings and walk-throughs to get started.

I explain each part of the process, and WHAT TO DO WHEN YOU'RE STUCK.

You'll also get tips on how to adjust the tools to your own context so that they work even better!

Watch the tutorials alongside using the planner, or bookmark the course page for whenever you need it.

Find tips, training & planning tools at

THEWRITEHABITPLANNER.COM/GETSTARTED

CREATIVE CREDIT. Content written, created, and designed by Dr Nicole Janz. Cover & Interior design by Dr Nicole Janz. Fonts and design elements used from Canva with licensed permission.
Photo of Dr Nicole Janz: Melanie Lal.

About Dr Nicole Janz

Like you, I struggled with daily writing and procrastination. Yet, I figured out a way to deal with both.

Fresh out of school I worked as a journalist. There was a daily deadline, a word count, and an editor waiting. The words came easily, and I thought I was a born writer...

Years later, as a Ph.D. student in Cambridge, that changed drastically. My dissertation felt like a huge mountain. My days had no structure. No one held me accountable. So I kept myself busy with *other* tasks and avoided my thesis. I ended up spending almost a year being ashamed, and I was deep in writer's block.

Have you ever been in a situation like that? Where you couldn't start, or felt like it's never going to be good enough?

But like you, I didn't give up. I broke down the mountain, removed the distractions, and created new habits and routines. Soon, the words flowed and writing became a joy. It felt easy again. Now, I have a system that not only worked for me, but I've shared this with hundreds of writers, and it's worked for them, too.

That's what *The Write Habit* is all about.

Use the planner to stay stay connected to your goals, keep refining your habits, and show up.

And on a rough day - remember that I believe in you!

You can do it! Just write.

Your coach,

Dr Nicole Janz

Made in the USA
Las Vegas, NV
14 December 2023